Los Angeles *Potpourri*

Los Angeles

Potpourri

Edited by
Tony Di Marco

Many of the photographs appearing in this
book, especially those of Downtown, City
Hall, Bunker Hill, Angels Flight, Wilshire
Boulevard and the Watts Towers, are the
work of photographer M. Richard Marx

Panoply Publications
NORTH HOLLYWOOD, CALIFORNIA

For information contact:
Panoply Publications
P. O. Box 2329
North Hollywood, CA 91610-0329

www.panoplypublications.com
e-mail: panoplypub@aol.com

ISBN 13:
978-0-9818391-3-4

ISBN 10:
0-9818391-3-4

Dedicated to all photographers of Los Angeles,
past, present and future

Contents

Preface

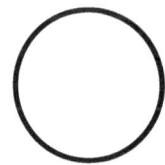

One of the definitions of "potpourri" is "A miscellaneous collection." That's exactly what *Los Angeles Potpourri* is — a miscellaneous collection of photographs that have one thing in common — they were all taken in Los Angeles. The book is not intended to be a historical account of the city, nor is it a collection of "then and now" photos. But it does have a touch of each of those topics as part of its ingredients. *Los Angeles Potpourri* is designed to give a look at parts of the city dating back to around 1860 up until about 100 years later, the 1960s, with a few photos made at a later date. There is no pattern to the pictures other than they're pretty much random views of some of the city's early landmarks and other vistas. They were taken back in the pre-digital photography days, when photographers had to carry huge view cameras plus all the necessary ancillary equipment — tripods, film holders, exposure meters and the like — to wherever they were going to make their pictures. As the years passed, cameras got smaller. View cameras eventually gave way to the hand-held 2.25" square negative camera like the Rolleiflex. And when 35mm cameras came into vogue, photographers of the day must have marveled at how lightly they could now travel. Many of the photos in this volume were done on a 4x5 view camera and/or a 2.25" roll film camera. Others were taken with a 35mm camera, most likely a Nikon. None were done with today's modern digital cameras. But enough with the photography lesson. The main purpose of this book is to house under one cover this collection of photographs of Los Angeles that otherwise would have languished in a dusty box for an untold number of years. Hopefully, now that they are somewhat organized, they will be enjoyed by nostalgia buffs and anyone else interested in the earlier days of the city.

We do not know the names of the intrepid photographers of the late 1800s who took the photographs that appear in the opening section of the book but they truly deserve a belated thanks for preserving the images of the many fascinating structures of early Los Angeles that have long ago been removed to make way for the growth of the modern city. Many of the other pictures in the book were taken by photographer M. Richard Marx, a native Angeleno who not only was a magnificent photographer but who also had a profound sense of history in compiling his work. Please see page 189 for a detailed biography of this unique camera artist. And if there's such a thing as icing on this cake it has to be the vast collection of vintage postcards that Jo Terrusa so kindly has let us use to close out the book.

We hope you enjoy this visit to Los Angeles.

1.
Old L. A.

**Some views of the city from around 1865
to the turn of the century**

The 1860s photo above is looking north on Main Street near the old junction with Spring and Temple Streets. This is now the heart of the Los Angeles Civic Center. Below is the Commercial Street business district around 1870.

North Main Street, above, around 1870. The Downey Block is at the extreme left and the Lafayette Hotel is the two story building in the center. Below is Main Street looking south from the Pico House in 1874. The Episcopal Church roof, Temple Block, First Congregational Church and the high school are beyond and above it.

When the Pico House at 430 N. Main in the Plaza was built in 1870 it was the city's finest hotel. It stood three-stories high, had about 80 rooms, baths on each floor and an interior courtyard. Pio Pico, the last Mexican governor of California, built the hotel, which is now a state Historical Landmark. Above, as it looked in 1875, below, in 2003.

Spring and Main Streets in 1880 — The "Temple Block." Looking south from Commercial Street.

Justice Street, looking north from Temple, in 1880.

The city is starting to show signs of growth in this view of Spring Street between First and Temple in the early 1880s. The streets are not paved but electric light poles are in place. The city was first lighted by electricity on December 31, 1882. Opponents to electricity claimed it "attracted bugs, contributed to blindness and had a bad effect on ladies' complexions!," according to Harris Newmark in his book, *"Sixty Years in Southern California."*

Top, looking north on Main Street from below Second Street in 1884. St. Vibiana's Cathedral, which was dedicated in 1876, is at right. In the middle photo, taken in 1890, several buildings have sprung up on the street including a gun store, flower shop and millenary shop next to the Cathedral. St. Vibiana's continued to function until damaged by the 1994 Northridge earthquake When the Archdiocese of Los Angeles built a new cathedral on Temple Street, St. Vibiana's was slated to be torn down but was given a reprieve and is now called Vibiana and serves as an event facility. It can be seen on the right in the 2010 photo below.

17

Above, the corner of Main and Third in 1884. The building was erected in the late 1870s and was torn down in 1905 to make way for the Citizens National Bank Building. The bottom photo is of downtown in the 1880s. Note the mode of transportation at the time: horse and carriage, bicycle, trolley and by foot. Automobiles were still a few years in the future. Bicycles and carriages took up most of the curbside parking.

South on Main and Spring at Temple Block around 1885. Trolleys were running but the streets were still unpaved and were dusty and dirty in the summer and muddy and difficult during the rainy season. It wasn't until August of 1887 that Main Street became the first paved street in Los Angeles.

Left: Spring Street in 1885 as it angled from First Street to meet Main at Temple.

Looking north from Second and Spring Streets in 1886.

Broadway looking north from Second Street in 1887. Note the still un-paved street.

Temple Block and vicinity north on Main Street in 1888. View is from the Federal Building site.

Main Street looking north from Temple in 1887. The tall mast in the center is the city's first electric light.

Above, Main Street in 1890, looking north. At the far right, the tower of St. Vibiana's Cathedral can be seen. Growth of the city is apparent.

Photo at right shows a minor landslide probably caused by rain. The street, in a residential neighborhood near downtown, is unpaved. The photo was taken circa 1885.

The corner of Second and Spring Streets about 1890. Note the overhead wires for electric lights and the two trolley tracks.

Spring Street around 1890. Traffic was light enough to allow those three gentlemen to carry on a conversation while standing in the street. But parking was starting to get a little difficult. Note the carriages parked curbside.

The post office at Main and Winston Streets in 1892.

Looking south on Broadway from Second Street, sometime between 1895 and 1901. Foot traffic, horse and carriage and trolleys were still the main modes of transportation.

Above, the Old Court House on Spring Street, 1895. Below, Spring Street from Third, also 1895.

Fifth and Broadway is packed with foot traffic in this 1900 shot. A bicyclist heads down the street and automobiles are still in the future.

Looking west on Second Street from Broadway circa 1900. A couple of lone pedestrians join the trolley cars and one horse and carriage in the middle of the block.

Sixth and Olive Streets in 1900.

Olive Street looking north from Third in 1900. The street is still not paved.

The automobile comes to Los Angeles. In this 1903 photo, several cars are parked on Broadway at Ninth Street and one gentleman tools down the street in his "convertible." Note the pot holes in the foreground that are in his direct line of travel. Hopefully they've been fixed by now. But at least the road looks like it is paved.

Figueroa Street at the corner of Adams in 1905.

LOS ANGELES POPULATION GROWTH

1781 - 44	1920 - 576,673
1800 - 315	1930 - 1,238,048
1820 - 650	1940 - 1,504,277
1850 - 1610	1950 - 1,970,358
1860 - 4385	1960 - 2,479,015
1870 - 5728	1970 - 2,816,061
1880 - 11,183	1980 - 2,966,850
1890 - 50,395	1990 - 3,485,398
1900 - 102,479	2000 - 3,694,820
1910 - 319,198	2010 - 4,065,585 (est.)

Los Angeles begins to take shape as a major city in this 1912 photo which is looking north from the southwest corner of Sixth and Hill Streets. Central Park, in the foreground, became what is now Pershing Square.

RANKING OF LOS ANGELES BY POPULATION
AMONG TOP TEN U.S. CITIES SINCE 1900

1900 - N/R	1980 - 3
1910 - N/R	1990 - 2
1920 - 10	2000 - 2
1930 - 5	2010 - 2
1940 - 5	
1950 - 4	(New York was #1 each
1960 - 3	decade and Chicago was #2 until passed by Los
1970 - 3	Angeles in 1990.)

2.

City Hall

Some random images of the city's most famous building

When the City Hall was completed in 1928 it was, by law, the tallest building in Los Angeles. While height restrictions for the city's buildings were relaxed in 1964, the City Hall, at 28 stories, is still an impressive and familiar site, especially in downtown L.A. The building was made a Los Angeles Historic-Cultural Monument in 1976. Most of these views were taken by photographer M. Richard Marx in the 1950s and 1960s.

3.

Downtown

Some views in and around the inner city

Avila House, above, on Olvera Street is the city's oldest surviving residence. The photos on this page and others in this chapter by M. Richard Marx were taken in 1953.

The Plaza Church

The Richfield Tower at 555 South Flower Street soon became a familiar downtown landmark after it was completed in 1929. The art deco building, which was designed by Stiles O. Clements, was 12 stories high and had a 130-foot tower which featured a large sign with the company's name on it. The building was colored in black and gold which represented the oil business. It was torn down in 1969 to make way for the ARCO Plaza complex.

The La Puma Bakery was located at 846 North Broadway and is pictured above, around 1919. The children in the middle photo, in 1923, are Providence La Puma, John La Puma and Martha La Puma, children of the La-Puma brothers, Marcantonio and Vito, who were owners of the bakery. The bakery building has expanded in size and now has two display windows in this photo. The bottom photo shows the Bank of America building at 850 North Broadway in 2010, which is where the bakery originally stood. The area is now the thriving center of the city's Chinatown.

Cole's is located at 118 East Sixth Street, Los Angeles 90014. It is open Monday-Wednesday from 11:30 a.m. until 10 p.m., Thursdays 11:30 a.m. until 11 p.m., Friday and Saturday 11:30 a.m. to 1:30 a.m. and 11:30 a.m. to 10 p.m. on Sundays.

So, who invented the French Dipped sandwich? These two downtown Los Angeles restaurants, both established in 1908, claim to be the originators of the unique sandwich. Cole's says that shortly after its opening a customer asked Jack Garlinghouse, the house chef, to dip the sandwich bun into the juice of the meat, thus creating a "dipped" sandwich. Philippe's says that while making a sandwich in 1918, Philippe Mathieu accidentally dropped the French roll onto the roasting pan filled with juice. The patron took the sandwich anyway and so was born Philippe's "French Dipped Sandwich." The answer to the question is still unknown but one thing is for certain — both restaurants offer a truly delicious sandwich.

Philippe's is located at 1001 North Alameda Street, Los Angeles 90012. Hours are 6 a.m. to 10 p.m. every day. Closed on Thanksgiving Day and Christmas Day.

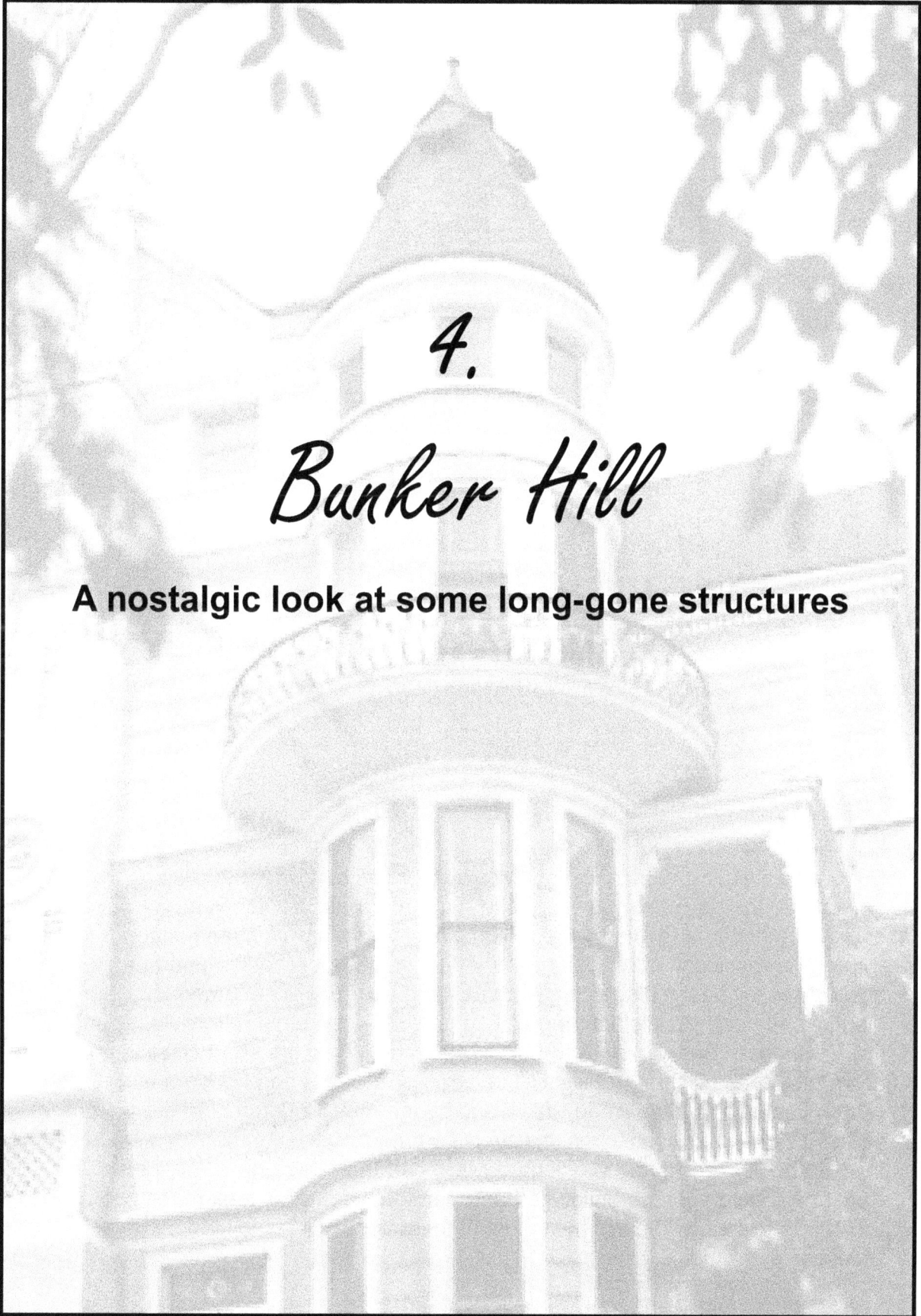

4.
Bunker Hill

A nostalgic look at some long-gone structures

Bunker Hill was one of Los Angeles' first real estate developments. Prudent Beaudry, an early L.A. businessman, saw the value of the property which was situated near the downtown area, above First and Hill Streets. Beaudry paid just over $500 for the land and by the 1870s it had become an affluent neighborhood, with grand mansions dotting the area. A few years later, hotels, apartments and businesses joined the single family homes and Bunker Hill became a thriving residential and business district. Angels Flight, a 315-foot cable railway that climbed up Hill Street to Bunker Hill, was built in 1901, mainly to transport citizens up and down the steep hillside. Bunker Hill became part of a federal government urban renewal campaign after World War II and by the mid-1960s most of the old properties had been removed to make way for commercial development that peaked in the 1980s. Photographer M. Richard Marx had the foresight to record the "old" Bunker Hill before all the buildings had been torn down. He took these photos in the 1950s and early 1960s, while most of them were still standing.

5.

Angels Flight

The Shortest Railroad in the World

Built in 1901 to connect downtown L.A. to the residential district on Bunker Hill, Angels Flight, 315 feet long, is known as the world's shortest railway. The two passenger cars originally made the trip for a nickel. The first Angels Flight was located at 3rd and Hill Streets. With the decline and ultimate razing of the structures on Bunker Hill in the 1960s, Angels Flight also became a candidate for the wrecker's ball but it was not demolished and instead was stored by the city for some 20 years. It was ultimately moved to 4th and Hill, re-opened briefly in 2001 and then closed again until March of 2010 when it was opened with a new drive system and brakes. The Angels Flight Railway Foundation now operates the system and it runs from 6:45 a.m. to 10 p.m., 7 days a week, 365 days a year. The fare is 25-cents each way. M. Richard Marx took these pictures in the late 1950s and early 1960s.

6.

In and Around

Exposition Park

With a look at the Coliseum and USC

An aerial view of central Los Angeles shows Exposition Park and the Coliseum and Sports Arena in the foreground. The City Hall and civic center can be seen on the right off in the distance.

The Coliseum under construction in 1922. The stadium opened in 1923.

The stadium sits ready to host the first Super Bowl game in 1967 which Green Bay won over Kansas City, 35-10. Attendance was far from a sellout at 63,036.

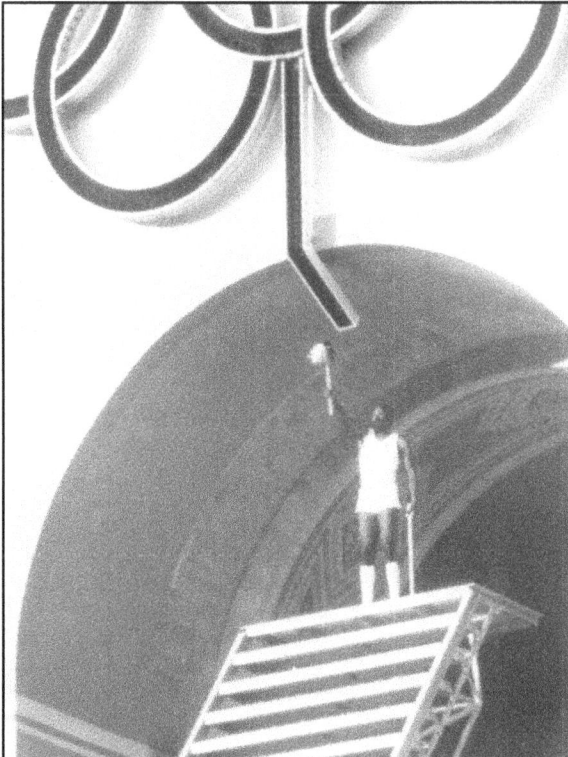

Among the many diversified events the Coliseum has hosted was the 1932 Olympic Games, above, and the 1984 Olympics. The opening day parade of nations in 1932 is in the top picture while famed UCLA athlete Rafer Johnson lights the torch to signify the opening of the 1984 games.

USC played football in the Coliseum for the first time in 1923. The Trojans and UCLA shared the Coliseum as their home football field from 1929 to 1982, after which the Bruins moved to the Rose Bowl. USC continues to play its home games in the famous stadium.

Perhaps the most exciting football game ever played in the Coliseum was the 1974 contest between USC and Notre Dame. At one point in the game the Trojans trailed 24-0 but they came back with 55 unanswered points to win the game.

The Los Angeles Dodgers played their home games in the Coliseum starting in 1958, while Dodger Stadium was being built in Chavez Ravine. Above, the opening ceremonies for the 1959 World Series, Dodgers vs. the Chicago White Sox.

The Coliseum that never was. In September, 1991, a $180-million renovation program was announced for the Coliseum. It was to begin in 1992, immediately following the Raiders' season and would be finished in time for the 1994 season. Some 200 luxury suites were to have been added along with a section of club seats just below the suites. A small upper deck seating section for general admission was to have been added but, otherwise, the familiar features of the stadium were to have remained unchanged. Capacity of the original 92,000-seat stadium would have been 85,000 for college games and about 70,000 for pro games. But these changes never came to be. The Raiders left Los Angeles in 1994 and USC remains the only football tenant in the venerable stadium, which is still among the most recognizable in the world.

In addition to the Coliseum and Sports Arena, Exposition Park is the site of several museums and other attractions.

The campus of the University of Southern California is just across the street from Exposition Park. Above, is Widney Hall, the oldest building on the Trojan campus. At right is the famed Tommy Trojan statue which stands in the middle of the campus.

Old College was one of the most familiar buildings on the USC campus before it was torn down in 1948 to make room for new classroom structures.

USC Chancellor Rufus B. von KleinSmid greets President Franklin D. Roosevelt in 1935.

USC's first athletic team in 1889. It is not known what sport or sports the above students represented nor if the bicycle was part of a sporting event or just a means of transportation. It is surmised that the young man in the cap and gown in the back row was either the first official Trojan student-athlete or possibly the team's learned coach.

Members of the 1913 championship Trojan track team look pretty spiffy in their suits and hats while driving down University Avenue.

Trojans on the 1936 Olympic track team included, left to right, front, Frank Wykoff and Foy Draper. Rear, Bill Graber, Harold Smallwood, Kenny Carpenter, Delos Thurber, Bill Sefton, Al Fitch, Earle Meadows and Roy Staley. The dapper gentleman in the beret is Coach Dean Cromwell, the greatest track and field coach of all time. Coach Cromwell's USC teams won 12 NCAA championships. He was the head track coach at USC from 1909 to 1948 (except for 1914 and 1915) and was head track coach of the USA Olympic team in 1948.

Waite Phillips Hall of Education, USC

Von KleinSmid Center for International and Public Affairs, USC

Eileen and Kenneth T. Norris Dental Science Center, USC

Hoffman Hall of Business Administration, USC

7.

Wilshire Boulevard

**A brief look at the famous street and then
a quick detour to Hollywood**

Anyone who remembers when the Bullocks Wilshire building housed a department store or when there was a May Co. Wilshire, Orbachs or Prudential Insurance building on the boulevard qualifies as a vintage Angeleno.

The May Co. building at Wilshire and Fairfax has been preserved and is now part of the L.A. museum system. Note the worker at left taking down the sign's letters. Below, the building the way it looks today.

Wilshire
Boulevard,
2010

ALEXANDER LIBERMAN
AMERICAN, 1912-

PHOENIX, 1974-1975
PAINTED STEEL

GIFT OF ANNA BING ARNOLD

When photographer M. Richard Marx saw this abstract sculpture entitled "Phoenix" by Alexander Liberman near the L.A. County Museum of Modern Art at 5095 Wilshire Boulevard, he decided to take a "few" pictures of the fascinating piece. What follows is a small selection of Marx's camera work.

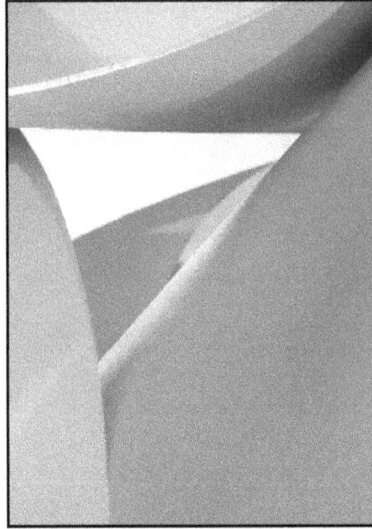

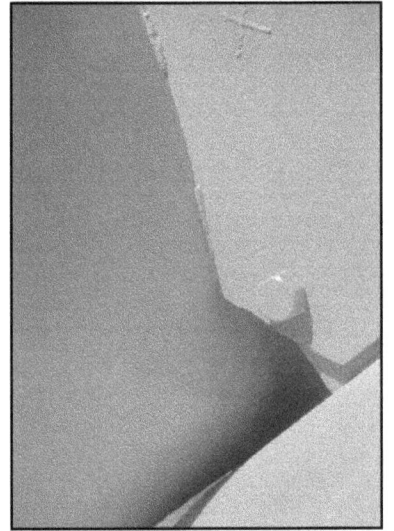

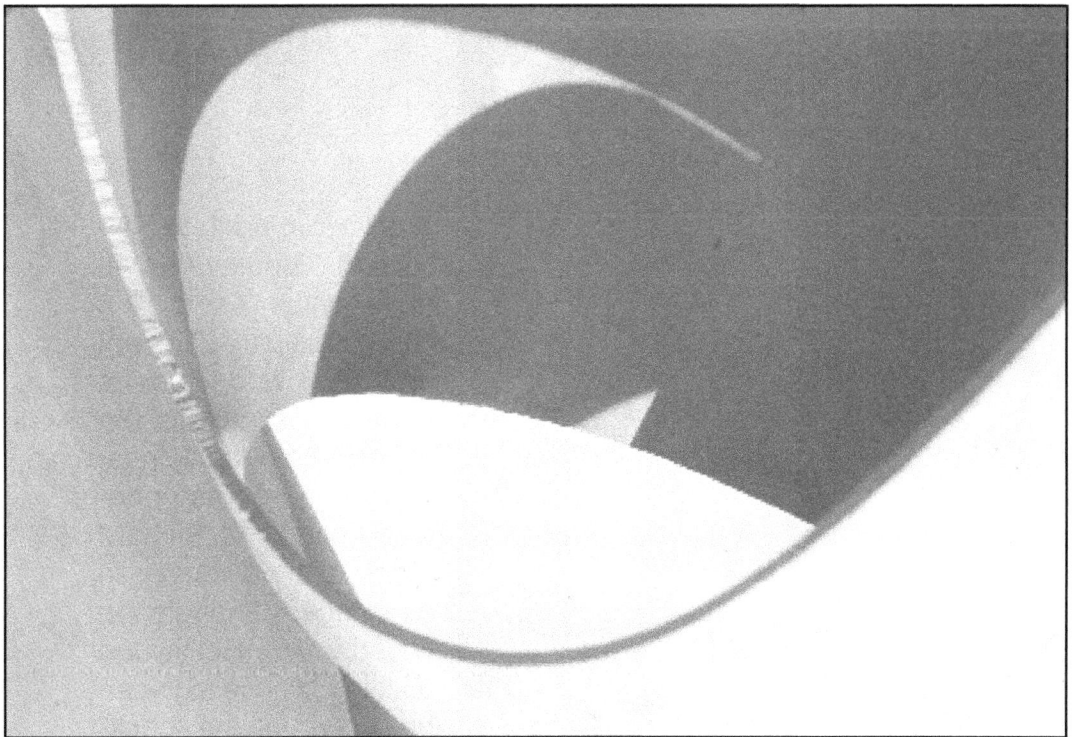

A quick run north to Hollywood Boulevard at night takes us to the NBC Studios at Sunset and Vine and Roberts Drive-In just across the street. Both buildings, shown here as photographed by M. Richard Marx, are no longer in existence, although the Broadway Hollywood building, whose sign can be seen in the background, below, is still standing.

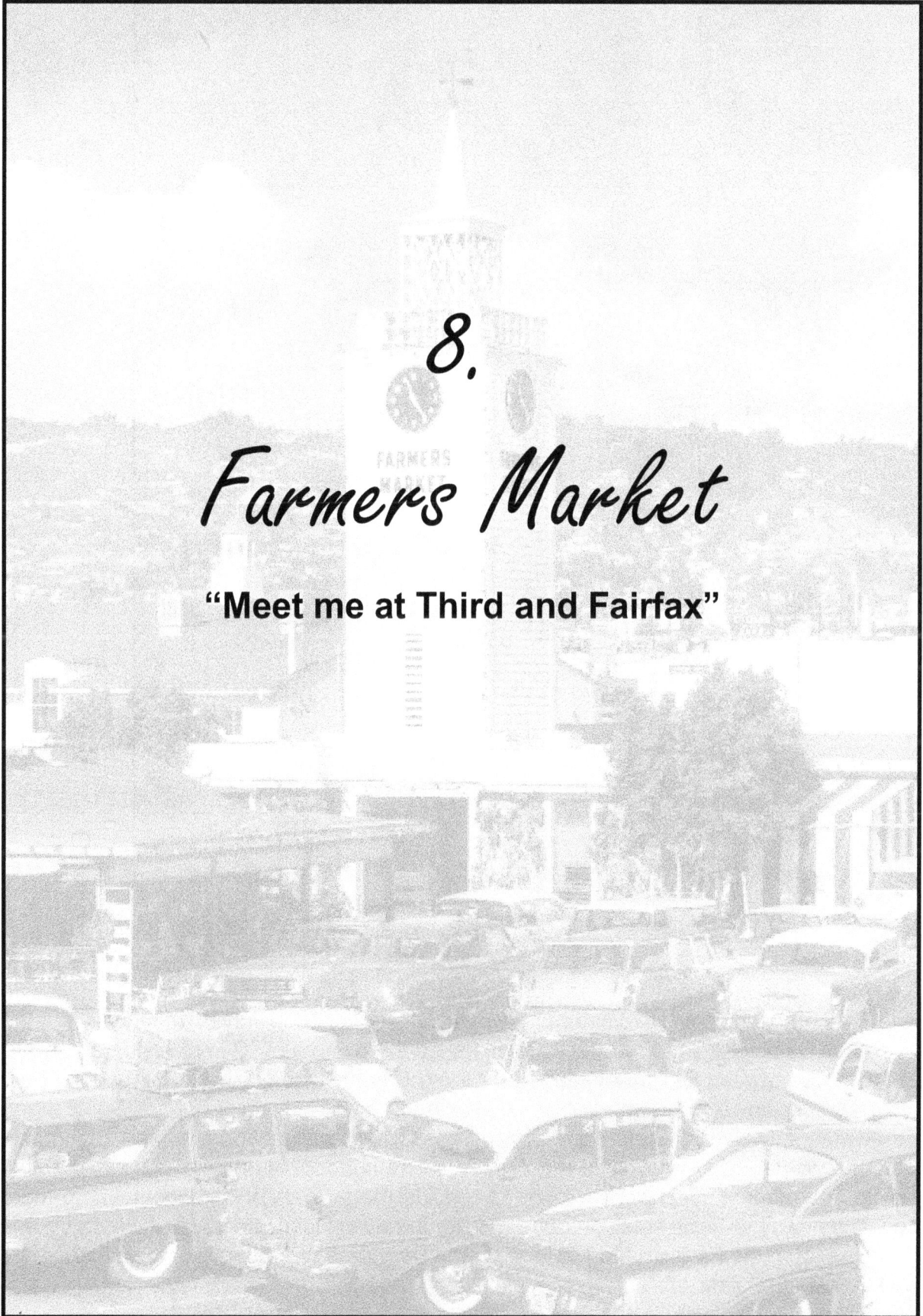

8.
Farmers Market

"Meet me at Third and Fairfax"

The Farmers Market, at Third and Fairfax, which first opened in July of 1934, was created by Roger Dahlhjelm and Fred Beck. They asked the owners of "Gilmore Island" on Fairfax Avenue between Beverly Boulevard and 3rd Street, if they could invite local farmers to park trucks on vacant Gilmore land to sell fresh produce to local shoppers. Some eighteen vendors, twelve of whom were farmers, responded to the opportunity and each paid 50-cents to park their trucks on the property. The concept was so popular that within months permanent stalls were erected to provide the farmers and vendors with a more convenient way to display their produce. The idea was an instant success and today, some 76 years later, the Farmers Market is still a thriving operation and Los Angeles landmark and tourist attraction.

136

The Market in 1936, just above 3rd Street at Fairfax. At the top of the photo is Gilmore Stadium, near the corner of Beverly Boulevard and Fairfax. The CBS Television Studios now occupy that site.

In addition to the Farmers Market and Gilmore Stadium, Gilmore Island was the site of Gilmore Field, the home of the Hollywood Stars Pacific Coast League baseball team. It was adjacent to Gilmore Stadium and opened in 1939. This view from center field shows the stands, which held about 13,000 fans. The area eventually became the home of CBS Television Studios, pictured below as viewed from Beverly Boulevard in 2010.

1935 — The Market on its first anniversary.

1940 — Wicker baskets on wheels were the official shopping carts. They eventually gave way to wooden versions which are still used today and are hand made in the Market's own carpentry shop. Once assembled, the contemporary carts are painted Farmers Market Green, the official designation of the color.

The Market has hosted events for visitors from its earliest days. The band, pictured at left, played at one of the first Fall Festival celebrations at the Market. The Fall Festival continues to this day and is so popular that fans call months in advance to determine the exact dates of the celebration.

Dick Kidson was one of the most beloved farmers at the Market. His stall, right, like most at the Market even to this day, was owner-operated, so customers were dealing with the owner when they shopped.

Within months after its opening the Market began serving food and, quickly, patios were furnished so diners could enjoy the outdoor setting and their meals.

A Gilmore gas station, "Earl's Service," shown here in 2010, has been replicated just off the Market's parking lot and is furnished exactly as it would have been in July of 1936.

At the turn of the present century the Market expanded with the addition of a new Plaza lined with shops and kiosks. To retain its link to the past the Market saved its taller Clock Tower to rise above the plaza. The Market's hours are 9 a.m. to 9 p.m. Monday through Friday, 9 a.m. to 8 p.m. Saturday, 10 a.m. to 7 p.m. on Sunday. Many merchants have extended hours.

PHOTOS COURTESY OF A. F. GILMORE CO.

9.

Watts Towers

Simon Rodia's Monument to Creativity

When Italian immigrant Simon Rodia began building what became known as the Watts Towers in 1921, he had no idea his work would become a National Historical Landmark that was regarded as a visual masterpiece. Rodia's sculptures are made from steel pipes, wire mesh and rods and mortar. They are embedded with pieces of glass, tile and other random objects. He worked on the towers in his spare time for 33 years, from 1921 to 1954. In 1955, Rodia moved to Martinez, California, and never returned. An engineering test performed by the city of Los Angeles proved the structures were safe and they were saved from demolition and ultimately deeded to the state of California. The Towers are located at 1765 East 107th Street in Los Angeles.

Photographer M. Richard Marx took these pictures of the Towers in 1963 and 1965.

145

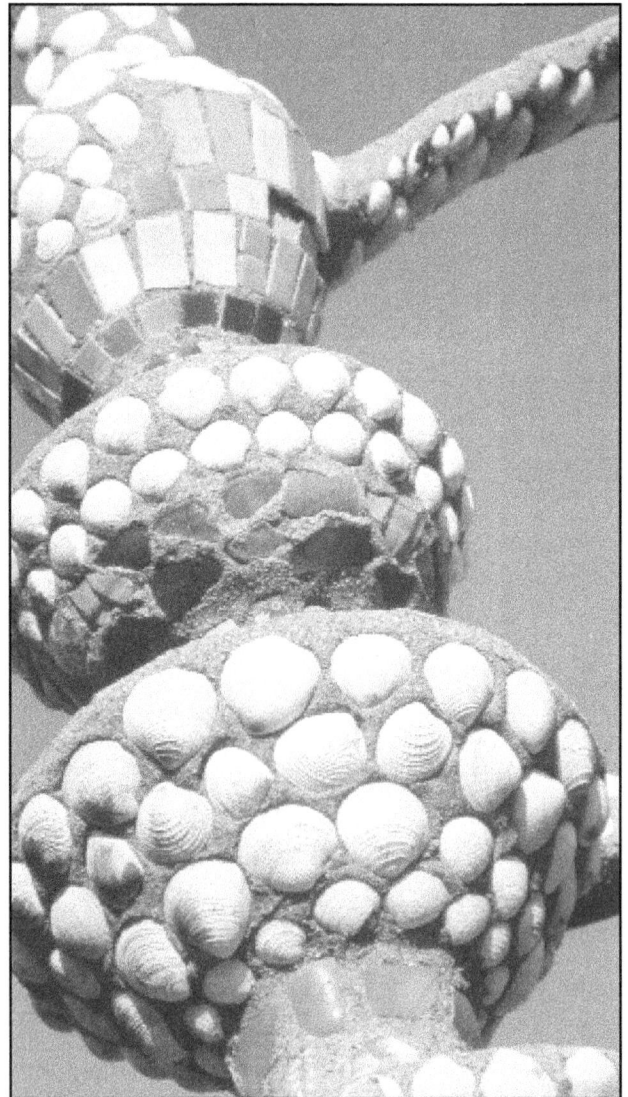

10.

The Studios

Have you ever heard of Edendale?

Today, Edendale is not much more than the name of a branch post office (90026) on Glendale Boulevard near Berkeley Avenue. It is situated just between the Silver Lake and Echo Park districts, but at one time it was the very heart of the motion picture industry in Los Angeles. This was early in the 1900s, when Edendale was the home of the Mack Sennett Studio, featuring the famous Keystone Cops, and a half-dozen other studios. They were all located on the part of Allesandro Street which today is Glendale Boulevard. The studios have all vanished into history with the exception of one building, a sound stage which was on the Mack Sennett lot and was declared a Historical Cultural Monument in 1982 by the city of Los Angeles. In the photo at right, top, is the Hornbeck Ranch, which was at 1712 Allesandro Street (now Glendale Boulevard) in 1906. This was the land on which the Sennett studio was built. The same area is shown in the lower photo in 1915 with the Sennett studio in full operation.

156

Above is the Mack Sennett Studio at 1712 Allesandro Street (now Glendale Boulevard) in Edendale in 1917. From 1909 to 1915 the studio was home of the New York Motion Picture Co., Bison and Keystone studios. In the middle photo, the last remaining building on the lot, the first all-concrete sound stage built in Los Angeles, is shown in 1980, when it was declared a Historical Monument. In the bottom photo the building is shown as it appeared in 2010.

157

The Mack Sennett Studios in Edendale in 1923, looking south-east.

Glendale Boulevard and Allessandro Street looking north in 1932.

The Selig Studio at 1845 Allesandro Street (now Glendale Boulevard) in 1909. It became the William Fox Studio in 1916, which was the forerunner of the 20th Century-Fox Studios.

Edendale in 1912. The Selig Studios are at the bottom left.

Reaguer Productions at 1745 Glendale Boulevard in Edendale, 1922. This was the site of the former Norbig Studio in 1915.

Looking north on Glendale Boulevard in 1980. Little remains of the studios that were on the street.

The original home of the Walt Disney Studios on Hyperion Avenue near Griffith Park Boulevard in Silver Lake in 1931. That's John Marshall High School in the background.

The Mabel Normand Studio at Bates and Effie Streets in East Hollywood in 1917. Mabel Normand was the premiere commedienne of the silent film era. This building became the William S. Hart Studio in 1918.

Aerial view of Hollywood in 1935 shows the RKO Studios and Paramount, on Melrose Avenue, in the foregound. Below is FBO (Film Booking Offices) at 780 Gower Street in 1926. This later became part of the RKO lot. Today it is the Paramount lot.

RKO Pictures lot on Melrose Avenue and Gower, shown in 1946. Paramount Studios, immediately next door going east, eventually absorbed the RKO lot.

The familiar Paramount Pictures main gate on Marathon Avenue in 1933, above, and in 1980, below.

Paramount kept its old gate, top, but added a double-arched new version at 5555 Melrose Avenue in 1981, middle photo. In the bottom picture is the Melrose gate as it appeared in 2010.

The Samuel Goldwyn Studios, foreground, shown in 1949. The site became Warners Hollywood Studio in 1980 and is now called, simply, The Lot. The street is Santa Monica Boulevard. The pie-shaped building near the top, left, at La Brea Avenue and near the huge gas storage tank, was the home of the DiMarco Winery, Hollywood's first and only winery beginning in 1934. The winery was located at 7112 Santa Monica Boulevard. The building was demolished years ago and the area is now a shopping center.

11.

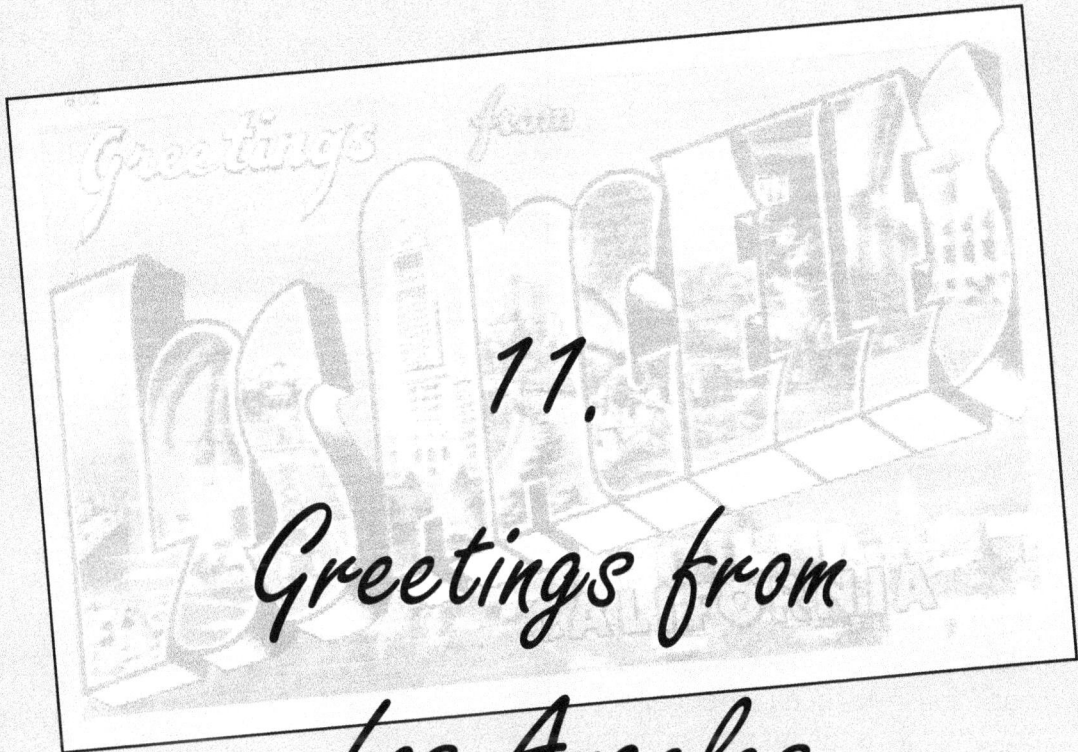

Greetings from
Los Angeles

Vintage postcards from the City of Angels

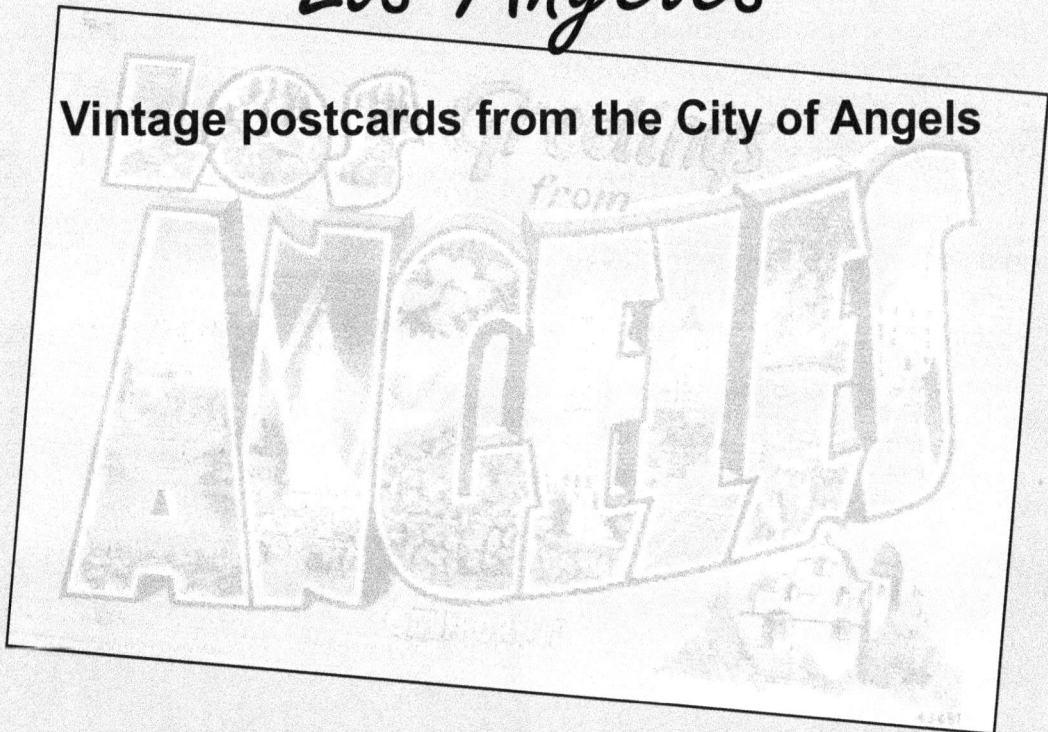

It was pure serendipity. When Jo Terrusa heard we were preparing *Los Angeles Potpourri*, she offered to give us a look at her collection of vintage Los Angeles postcards. We were overwhelmed. It was an absolutely sensational collection of cards that went back to the early 1900s and even beyond — exactly the type of material we were looking for to include in this book. Jo graciously loaned us her collection and gave us permission to pick out cards for this chapter of the book. It was a daunting task, because her fascinating collection deserves a book of its own, but we're including a representative selection of her cards that we hope you will enjoy as much as we did in selecting them. We thank Jo so very much for her generosity in sharing her fine collection with us.

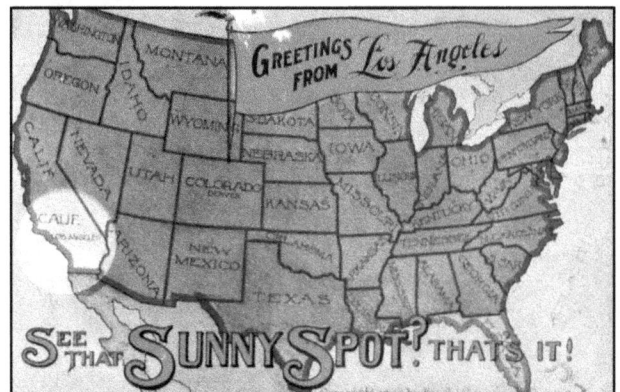

It's not surprising that the City Hall is the most familiar building in the city because it easily is the most photographed. These are just a few postcards featuring the building. Some say "The *New* City Hall," which means they date back to around 1928, when the building was completed.

169

Los Angeles County Court House

8227. Los Angeles County Court House and Hall of Records.

HALL OF RECORDS, AND COUNTY COURT HOUSE, LOS ANGELES, CALIFORNIA

LA. 26—New Post Office and Federal Building—and City Hall, Los Angeles, California

The former City Hall is on the card top, left. Top right is the County Court House, also shown in the middle cards. Bottom left is the new Post Office and Federal Building and the City Hall. The building, bottom, right, is the Hall of Justice.

Top, left, South Broadway at 7th looking south; center, 6th Street showing First Methodist Church; right, Spring Street looking north from 8th. Middle, left, Broadway at 7th looking north; right, Broadway at night. Next row, left, looking west at 7th and Hill; right, Wilshire Boulevard, Bullocks at left, Town House at right. Bottom, Western Avenue north from Wilshire.

171

Hotel Lankershim, 700 S. Broadway

Hotel Tahoe, 1043 W. 6th Street

Hotel Tyler, Grand Avenue at 38th

Clark Hotel, 426 S. Hill Street

Hotel Trinity, 851 S. Grand

Biltmore Hotel, 506 S. Grand

Ambassador Hotel, 3400 Wilshire

Hotel Hayward, 601 S. Spring

Rosslyn Hotel, 5th and Main

Gates Hotel, 6th, Figueroa and Wilshire

Hotel Cecil, Main Street between 6th and 7th

Hotel Hollywood, Hollywood Boulevard and Highland, 1911

Hotel Alexandria restaurant, 501 S. Spring Street

Ye Bull Penn Inn, Mayflower Hotel, 535 S. Grand Avenue

Lady's reception room, Van Nuys Hotel, 103 W. 4th Street

Eastern-Columbia, Broadway at 9th

Sears on 9th Street

J. W. Robinson Co., 7th and Grand

Bullock's, Broadway, Hill and 7th.

Barker Brothers, 7th and Flower

174

Trinity Auditorium, 9th and Grand

Shrine Auditorium, 665 W. Jefferson

Auditorium, 5th and Olive, 1910

Auto Club, Figueroa and Adams, 1927

Jonathon Club, 545 S. Figueroa Street

Downtown city view, 1908

Hellman Bank promotional card

175

L.A. Central Library, 630 W. 5th Street

Los Angeles Times, 202 W. 1st Street

Union Station, 800 N. Alameda Street

Downtown from the Huntington Building

CBS on Sunset Boulevard, Hollywood

NBC, Sunset and Vine, Hollywood

Hollywood Bowl

Lobby, YMCA

Wilshire Boulevard Congregational Church

German Lutheran Church

Church of the Immaculate Conception, 9th and Valencia Streets

The Rector and Choir, Christ Episcopal Church

St. Vibiana's

St. Vincent's

Exposition Park entrance, 1922

Museum and Gardens, Exposition Park

Aerial view, Exposition Park, Coliseum

Coliseum, 1923

Westlake Park palm drive, 1909

Westlake Park boathouse, 1916

Westlake Park, 1907

Lake View Hotel, Westlake Park, 1915

Echo Park Playground, 1914

Echo Park, 1916

Moonlight at Eastlake Park, 1912

Selig Zoo entrance, Eastlake Park, 1917

Entrance to Elysian Park

Tunnels through Elysian Park

Picnic grounds in Griffith Park

Planetarium, Griffith Park

Central Park (Pershing Square), 1916

Soldier's Monument, Central Park

Fountain in Central Park, 1915

Midwinter day in Pershing Square

Pershing Square and apartment house district

Pershing Square

Looking north across Pershing Square

Looking southwest

The State Normal School, located on what is now the site of the Central Library at 630 W. 5th Street. The school eventually became the southern branch of the Universtiy of California, and moved to a location on Vermont and Melrose Avenues, where LACC is today. Then the school's name was changed to UCLA and the new, present day campus was built in Westwood.

Manual Arts High School

Lincoln High School

Polytechnic High School

Los Angeles High School

The Union High School, Hollywood

181

Old Mission Plaza Church

Temple Block, Spring and Main Streets

Chester Place, 1908

DeLongpre kiosk and residence, 1910

Arthur Letts home, Hollywood

Bernheimer Bros. Japanese bungalow

Dr. A. G. Castle's mansion, Hollywood

A log cabin, Los Angeles, 1912

A home in Hollywood, 1915

Grauman's Chinese Theater, Hollywood

Hollywood Boulevard at night

Van de Kamp's Holland Dutch Bakery Windmill Store #1

Oil Fields, 1914

Hollywood Dam, Lake Hollywood

West Adams Boulevard

183

Cafe Bristol, 4th and Spring Streets

The Victor Hugo, 1929

The Italian Village, 425 W. 8th Street

The Chocolate Shop, 207 W. 5th Street

Lucca Restaurant, 501 S. Western

The Wagon Wheel, 1325 W. 7th Street

Ontra Cafeteria, 757 S. Vermont Avenue

Philippe's, 1001 N. Alameda Avenue

Olvera Street

Glendale Boulevard-Hyperion viaduct

King's Tropical Inn, Washington and Adams Boulevards

El Patio Ballroom, 3rd and Vermont

Olvera Street

Citizens Trust & Savings Bank, 736 S. Hill

185

University of Southern California, 1911

University of Southern California, 1922

West Adams Boulevard

Figueroa Street

Angels Flight

The Plaza

The Public Library, Hollywood

La Grande Station, Santa Fe Railroad

1201—Spring Street, Los Angeles, California.

Jo Terrusa's collection of vintage postcards is unique because of the wide selection of pictorial subjects on the front of them. But equally intriguing are the messages written on the cards. Most correspondents enjoyed Los Angeles. They were particularly impressed by the weather, with many sending cards in the winter and pointing out that they were enjoying sunny, warm days. But the most prophetic comment on the cards was made on the one pictured above. The writer, who just signed his initials, "M.N.A.," in this card that he addressed to Mr. W. L. Anderson of Ashville, North Carolina, wrote, *"This is a very busy city."* The card was mailed in July of 1907, more than one hundred years ago. "M.N.A.," you should see us now!

About M. RICHARD MARX

Versatility is the key word in describing the photography of M. Richard Marx, whose work makes up a good portion of this book. A true artist with the camera, he was equally at home in the field or in the studio. In the darkroom his creativity was enhanced by his technical skills in composing and printing the literally thousands of color and black and white photographs he took over a career that spanned more than half a century.

Born in Los Angeles, California on January 31, 1915, Marx spent his youth in L.A. and in San Francisco. He went east to attend college and he was a classmate of actor-dancer Gene Kelly at the University of Pittsburgh.

After college he returned to Los Angeles and worked in retail sales before becoming an assistant to Tom Kelly, famous as the photographer of the Marilyn Monroe calendar. After a year with Kelly, Marx began freelancing and did advertising photography for companies such as Eastman Kodak, DuPont, GAF (Agfa) and Wollensak Optical. He was in the army during World War II and in 1948 he married Beatrice Luce, who became his assistant during his many photography projects.

Dick and Bea made countless photo junkets to Mexico, Europe, North Africa, Asia and the U.S. and Canada over the years, where he recorded thousands of outstanding images which are part of his vast inventory of both color and black and white photographs.

He contributed to such magazines as Sunset and House Beautiful, wrote a travel photography column for Westways Magazine and wrote and illustrated two books, "About Mexico's Children" and "Printing With Variable Contrast Papers." He had showings of his work at several museums and galleries and his photos of Mexico have been used to illustrate the Mexican section of Compton's Encyclopedia.

The peripatetic photographer turned to teaching later in his career and he taught photography at East Los Angeles College for 14 years before retiring as professor emeritus.

M. Richard Marx died in Los Angeles on May 22, 1999 at the age of 84. His artistic versatility left behind a true legacy of enduring and outstanding photography and we are pleased to present some of his work in this book.

PICTURE CREDITS

Credits for the pictures from left to right are separated by a semi-colon; from top to bottom by dashes.

FRONT COVER: Donna DiMarco. 11 , ASP. 12, ASP (American Stock Photos) -- ASP. 13, ASP -- ASP. 14, ASP -- Trans Media Images (TMI). 15, ASP -- ASP. 16, ASP. 17, ASP -- ASP -- TMI. 18, ASP -- ASP. 19, ASP. 20, ASP -- ASP. 21, ASP -- ASP. 22, ASP. 23, ASP -- ASP. 24, ASP. 25, ASP -- ASP. 26, ASP. 27, ASP -- ASP. 28, ASP -- ASP. 29, ASP -- ASP. 30, ASP. 31, ASP. 32, ASP. 33, T.M.I. 34, Overland Monthly -- M. Richard Marx. 35, Donna DiMarco. 36, Marx -- Marx. 37, Marx -- Marx. 38, Marx -- Marx. 39, Marx. 40, Marx -- Marx. 41, Marx; Marx -- Marx. 42, Marx. 43, Marx; Marx -- Marx. 44, Marx; T.M.I. -- M. Richard Marx; Marx. 45, Marx. 46, Marx -- Marx. 47, Marx. 48, M. Richard Marx -- Marx; Marx. 49, Marx. 50, Marx - Marx -- Marx. 51, Marx. 52, T.M.I. 53, M. Richard Marx. 54, Marx -- Marx; Marx. 55, Joseph G. LaPuma Collection -- Joseph G. LaPuma Collection -- T.M.I. 56, T.M.I. -- T.M.I. 57, M. Richard Marx -- Marx. 58, Marx. 59, T.M.I. -- T.M.I. 60, M. Richard Marx -- Marx. 61, Marx -- Marx; Marx. 62. Marx -- Marx; Marx. 63, Marx. 64, M. Richard Marx. 65, Marx -- Marx. 66, Marx -- Marx. 67, Marx -- Marx. 68, Marx; Marx -- Marx -- Marx. 69, Marx. 70, Marx -- Marx; Marx. 71, Marx. 72, Marx -- Marx. 73, Marx; Marx -- Marx; Marx. 74, Marx; Marx -- Marx. 75, Marx -- Marx. 76, Marx; Marx -- Marx. 77, Marx; Marx -- Marx; Marx. 78, Marx -- Marx. 79, Marx; Marx; Marx -- Marx. 80, Marx -- Marx. 81, Marx. 82, Marx -- Marx. 83, Marx; Marx; Marx -- Marx. 84, Marx -- Marx; Marx. 85, Marx; Marx -- Marx; Marx. 86, Marx -- Marx. 87, Marx; Marx -- Marx. 88, Marx -- Marx; Marx; Marx. 89, Marx -- Marx. 90, Marx -- Marx; Marx. 91, Marx-- Marx; Marx. 92, Marx; Marx -- Marx; Marx -- Marx. 93, Marx -- Marx; Marx -- Marx; Marx. 94, Marx -- Marx. 95, Marx; Marx -- Marx; Marx -- Marx. 96, Marx -- Marx; Marx. 97, Marx -- Marx. 98, Marx -- Marx. 99, Marx. 100, M. Richard Marx -- Marx. 101, Marx. 102, Marx; Marx -- Marx. 103, Marx -- Marx; Marx; Marx. 104, Marx; Marx -- Marx. 105, Marx -- Marx. 106, Marx -- Marx; Marx. 107, Marx -- Marx; Marx. 108, Marx -- Marx. 109, Marx -- Marx. 110, Marx -- Marx. 111, T.M.I. 112, L.A. Memorial Coliseum. 113, T.M.I. 114, L.A. Memorial Coliseum -- L.A. Memorial Coliseum. 115, Amateur Athletic Foundation Library -- Amateur Athletic Foundation Library. 116, Republic Federal Collection -- U.S.C. Sports Information Department. 117, Los Angeles Dodgers -- T.M.I. 118, Los Angeles Memorial Coliseum -- Los Angeles Memorial Coliseum -- Los Angeles Memorial Coliseum. 119, T.M.I. -- T.M.I. 120, Republic Federal Collection -- Republic Federal Collection. 121, Republic Federal Collection -- Republic Federal Collection. 122, Republic Federal Collection. 123, Republic Federal Collection -- Republic Federal Collection. 124, All, Republic Federal Collection. 125, Marx. 126, T. M.I. 127, M. Richard Marx. 128, Marx -- T.M.I. 129, Marx -- Marx. 130, T.M.I. -- T.M.I.; T.M.I.; T.M.I. -- T.M.I.; T.M.I. 131, M. Richard Marx -- Marx. 132, Marx; Marx; Marx -- Marx; Marx; Marx -- Marx; Marx; Marx. 133, Marx -- Marx. 134, Marx -- Marx. 135, A. F. Gilmore Co. 136, A. F. Gilmore Co. 137, A. F. Gilmore Co. 138, A. F. Gilmore Co. -- T.M.I. 139, A. F. Gilmore Co. -- A. F. Gilmore Co. 140, A. F. Gilmore Co. -- A. F. Gilmore Co. 141, A. F. Gilmore Co. -- T.M.I. 142, A. F. Gilmore Co. 143, M. Richard Marx. 144, Marx -- Marx. 145, Marx; Marx. 146, Marx. 147, Marx -- Marx -- Marx -- Marx. 148, Marx. 149, Marx -- Marx. 150, Marx; Marx -- Marx. 151, Marx. 152, Marx -- Marx; Marx. 153, Marx; Marx -- Marx. 154, Marx -- Marx. 155, T.M.I. 156, Marc Wanamaker/Bison Archives -- Marc Wanamaker/Bison Archives. 157, Marc Wanamaker/Bison Archives -- T.M.I. -- T.M.I. 158, Marc Wanamaker/Bison Archives -- Marc Wanamaker/Bison Archives. 159, Marc Wanamaker/Bison Archives -- Marc Wanamaker/Bison Archives. 160, Marc Wanamaker/Bison Archives -- T.M.I. 161, Marc Wanamaker/Bison Archives -- Marc Wanamaker/Bison Archives. 162, Marc Wanamaker/Bison Archives-- Marc Wanamaker/Bison Archives. 163, Marc Wanamaker/Bison Archives. 164, Marc Wanamaker/Bison Archives -- T.M.I. 165, T.M.I. -- T.M.I. -- T.M.I. 166, Marc Wanamaker/Bison Archives. 167-187, Postcards from the private collection of Jo Terrusa. BACK COVER: M. Richard Marx; Donna DiMarco; M. Richard Marx -- T.M.I.; Jo Terrusa Collection.

MORE BOOKS FROM PANOPLY PUBLICATIONS

THE DAYS I KNEW
By Lillie Langtry
The autobiography of the famous English actress and Victorian beauty.
ISBN 1-886571-13-9
Softcover, 287 pages
$21.95

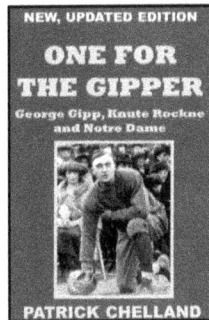

ONE FOR THE GIPPER
By Patrick Chelland
The biography of George Gipp of Notre Dame. Updated, 3rd edition.
ISBN 978-0-9818391-0-3
Softcover, 298 pages
$24.95

THE CALIFORNIA WINERY GUIDE
Names and addresses of over 3000 California wineries plus websites, labels and more. Full color.
ISBN 978-1-886571-26-6
Softcover, 264 pages
$49.95

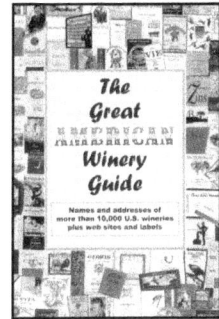

THE GREAT AMERICAN WINERY GUIDE
Listings of more than 10,000 American wineries by state. Fully indexed.
ISBN 978-0-9818391-1-0
Softcover, 240 pages
$24.95

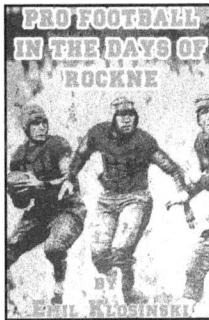

PRO FOOTBALL IN THE DAYS OF ROCKNE
By Emil Klosinski
A fascinating account of pro football before the days of the NFL.
ISBN 1-886571-14-7
Softcover, 175 pages
$16.95

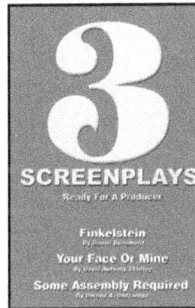

3 SCREENPLAYS READY FOR A PRODUCER
By Beaumont, Stanley and Gazzaniga
Comedy, mystery and parody in movie script form.
ISBN 1-886571-22-8
Softcover, 329 pages
$24.95

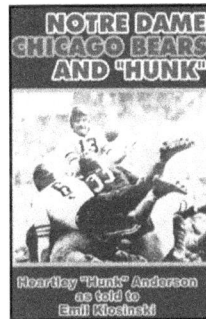

NOTRE DAME, CHICAGO BEARS AND "HUNK"
By Anderson and Klosinski
The amazing life story of football icon Heartley "Hunk" Anderson.
ISBN 1-886571-20-1
Softcover, 252 pages
$19.95

ARROW ARROW
By Daniel Beaumont
A page turner with bizarre characters and unexpected twists and turns.
ISBN 1-88651-17-1
Softcover, 287 pages
$19.95

THE THREE KEYS
By Tony DiMarco
Illustrated by Dania Mallette
A delightful adventure story for children 7-12.
ISBN 978-0-98918391-2-7
Softcover, 143 pages
$9.95

ORDER ON-LINE AT www.amazon.com OR Barnes & Noble www.bn.com OR FROM YOUR FAVORITE BOOKSTORE

www.ingramcontent.com/pod-product-compliance
Lightning Source LLC
Chambersburg PA
CBHW080504110426
42742CB00017B/2995